D0760315

# Amazing Pranks & Blunders

**Peter Eldin**
**Illustrated by Kim Blundell**

 Sterling Publishing Co., Inc.   New York

**LIBRARY OF CONGRESS**
**Library of Congress Cataloging-in-Publication Data**

Eldin, Peter.
   Amazing pranks & blunders / by Peter Eldin : illustrated by Kim
Blundell.
      p. cm.
   Includes index.
   Summary: An illustrated collection of anecdotes describing a variety of
pranks, hoaxes, frauds, humorous mistakes, practical jokes, goofs, and
slip-ups.
   ISBN 0-8069-6884-2
   1. American wit and humor. 2. Wit and humor, Juvenile. (1. Wit and
humor.) I. Blundell, Kim, ill. II. Title: Amazing pranks and blunders.
PN6163.E43 1988
818'.5402—dc 19

*A Special Willowisp Press, Inc. Edition*

Published in 1988 by Sterling Publishing Co., Inc.
Two Park Avenue, New York, New York 10016
The material in this book was compiled and adapted
from *Amazing Blunders and Bungles* and
*Amazing Hoaxes and Frauds* published in Great Britain
by Octopus Books Limited.

Copyright © 1987 by Octopus Books Limited
Distributed in Canada by Oak Tree Press Ltd.
% Canadian Manda Group, P.O. Box 920, Station U
Toronto, Ontario, Canada M8Z 5P9
Printed in the United States
10 9 8 7 6 5 4 3 2 1
ISBN 0-87406-460-0

# Contents

**By the Same Author**
Amazing Ghosts & Other Mysteries

# To the Reader

**D**id you hear about the prisoners who dug a tunnel out of their cell—straight into a courtroom? Or the bride who got married—to the best man? Or about the world's most goofed-up secret weapon?

Well, nobody's perfect! We humans can make the most hilarious mistakes and miscalculations, and we can be taken in by the most obvious frauds! This book is full of the funniest blunders ever—botched robberies, unbelievable slip-ups, outrageous scams, con games and pranks (like the one Frank Sinatra played on Mel Brooks).

Could you have been taken in by the sting?

Could you have made the mistake?

Read on—and find out!

# 1 · They Got Away With It

## Great Forger

Alceo Dossena was so good at forging sculptures that some experts thought his works were better than the originals. In the 1920s, Dossena fakes were to be found in most of the great museums of the world—although the curators did not know their prized possessions were clever forgeries. In fact, Dossena was such a superb craftsman that although some of his works have been discovered and exposed, it is very likely that many of his sculptures are still on display in major collections and believed to be genuine.

7

# Too Many Monas

On August 21, 1911, one of the world's most famous paintings, the *Mona Lisa*, was stolen from the Louvre in Paris. In the following six months at least six wealthy Americans bought what they thought was the genuine *Mona Lisa*, but they were all fakes, painted by master forger, Yves Chaudron. The frauds did not make Chaudron any wealthier, however. All the money he made was stolen by one of his accomplices.

# Too Easy

The great scientist Albert Einstein visited many universities giving talks about his theory of relativity.

One day his chauffeur said, "Dr. Einstein, I've heard you deliver your talk about 30 times. I know it by heart and I bet I could even give a talk on relativity myself."

"Well," said Einstein, "I'll give you the chance at the next university. They don't know me there so you can give the talk."

When they reached the university, Einstein pretended to be the chauffeur, and the chauffeur, pretending to be Einstein, gave the talk.

The chauffeur's lecture was word perfect and none of the university professors realized they had

*They Got Away With It* 9

been fooled. The ruse was almost discovered, however, when the chauffeur was about to leave. One of the professors asked him a very complex question that involved mathematical equations and formulas. The poor man had no idea what the answer was, but he thought quickly.

"The answer to your question is quite simple," he said. "In fact, it is so easy, I'm going to ask my chauffeur to come and answer it for you."

## Eye—for a Buck

Lama Lobsang Rampa wrote a number of successful books about his life in a Tibetan monastery. In the books, he told of a miraculous "third eye" which he possessed that gave him a unique spiritual insight.

But Lama Lobsang Rampa never existed and neither did the monastery. The books were created by Cyril Henry Hoskins who made a lot of money from them.

# The Queen's Psychiatrist

**B**aron David James Rothschild was psychiatrist to Queen Juliana of the Netherlands until 1978. It was then revealed that he was a fraud. In reality he was a Dutch laborer called Henry de Vries.

# Trying to Get Out of the Bath

**D**uring World War I the writer H. L. Mencken wrote a joke article on the history of the bathtub in America. Titled "A Neglected Anniversary," it appeared in the *New York Evening Mail* on December 28, 1917.

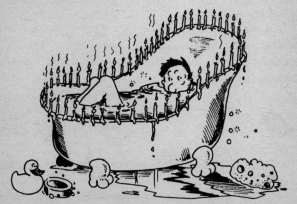

Much to Mencken's surprise the article was accepted as genuine, and it was not long before the "facts" he had invented for a laugh were being quoted by other people in serious articles about bathing.

Several years later, Mencken thought that the hoax had gone far enough. He wrote a feature pointing out that he had invented the history, but the joke had now gotten out of hand. This article appeared in several newspapers on May 23, 1926, but in spite of it, Mencken's invented facts continued to be quoted for over 35 years!

## The Greatest Liar on Earth

In an article in the magazine, *Wide World*, published in 1898, Louis de Rougement described how he had spent 30 years living with cannibals in northwestern Australia after he had been shipwrecked.

He told how he had participated in cannibal feasts and how he had built himself a house of pearl shells. He also described how he had cured himself of fever by sleeping inside a dead buffalo, and he claimed to have ridden on the backs of 600-pound turtles.

He became an instant celebrity and received numerous invitations to talk to scientific societies about his adventures. So famous were his exploits

that a model of him was placed in Madame Tussaud's, the famous waxwork gallery in London. When he was eventually exposed as a fraud however, he wasn't phased. He made the most of the situation by touring South Africa as "the Greatest Liar on Earth."

## Magnetic Money

A U.S. con man once stole a great deal of money from a bank by means of a surprisingly simple trick. He opened an account at the bank and was given a supply of deposit slips. These were printed with his account number in magnetic

ink. Knowing that the computer picked up magnetic ink and not ordinary ink, the man simply went to the bank, removed the loose deposit slips that had been stacked at the counters for the use of customers, and substituted the slips bearing his account number. No matter what account number people wrote on the slip, the computer picked up his number printed in magnetic ink. After three days the con man closed his account and got away with $100,000!

# 2 · Practical Jokes of the Rich & Famous

## Sinatra's Practical Joke

Film producer Mel Brooks was delighted when Frank Sinatra allowed him to borrow his studio trailer to entertain a friend. Brooks, new to Hollywood, was filled with gratitude that the star had been kind enough to offer his help.

After a few drinks, Mel Brooks and his friend felt they needed a breath of fresh air so they stepped out of the trailer for a walk. When they got outside, they were astonished to find that they did not know where they were. Sinatra had hired a truck to take the trailer to a side street miles away. It was some time before Mel Brooks found his way back to the studio!

# How Heavy *Was* Brando?

In one scene in the film *The Godfather*, actor Marlon Brando was supposed to be injured and had to be carried away on a stretcher.

When the scene was being filmed, the actors found they could hardly lift the stretcher. It had suddenly become extremely heavy. Brando had secretly loaded it with several very heavy weights.

## Beware of Dutch Elms

Scientists have been searching for a cure for the common cold for a long time. It seemed that the breakthrough came in 1973 when a Dr. Clothier announced on a British radio station that powdered Dutch elm cured the common cold.

There appeared to be some unusual side effects to the cure, however, Clothier reported. One scientist, after treating himself with powdered Dutch elm, caught Dutch elm disease. As a result, his red hair had turned yellow and he had eventually gone bald. Dr. Clothier therefore warned all red-haired listeners not to use this remedy and to avoid any areas where Dutch elm disease was present. Dr. Clothier was, in reality, comedian, Spike Milligan.

## Shame on You, Oliver Reed!

The English actor Oliver Reed, visiting the U.S., was staying at a hotel that had a large goldfish tank in its reception area. He obtained a carrot and cut it into the shape of a goldfish. Then, when all attention was upon him, he walked to the fish tank, put his hand in, brought out the carrot and ate it. It was an old theatrical gag, but the management did not appreciate the joke. They ordered the actor to leave the hotel.

# Douglas Fairbanks' Last Laugh

Douglas Fairbanks, the film star, promised four close friends that they would receive something in his will when he died. But when the will was read after Fairbanks' death in 1939, there was no mention of anything left to them.

Two months later, Douglas Fairbanks, Jr. asked the four to come and see him. He gave each of them an envelope containing a check for $60,000. His father had left the four out of his will—just for a laugh.

# No Laughs for Lasky

Film pioneer Jesse Lasky was proud of his ability to deliver a good speech at a moment's notice. One day, he accepted an invitation from cinema owner Sid Grauman to talk to a group of film distributors about the state of the industry.

When he walked onto the floodlit stage, he was disappointed at the lack of applause. He started with a witty introduction designed to make the audience laugh, but they didn't make a sound.

Undeterred, Lasky continued with his hour-long speech, but it was hard going—for he received absolutely no reaction from the audience. Even at the end of the speech, there was no applause.

Then the lights went up and Lasky discovered that the entire audience was made up of wax dummies!

# Paul Newman Gets Even

Film director Robert Altman wondered what on earth had happened when hordes of people turned up at his home for a party. The guests had received invitations, but Altman knew nothing about the party.

A short while later he was inundated with people who wanted to be cast in his next film. A local television station had announced that he was looking for 2,500 extras.

Then he found out who was behind the hoax. It was actor Paul Newman. When the two men had worked together on the film *Buffalo Bill and the Indians*, Altman had filled Newman's on-location trailer with popcorn, as a joke. Paul Newman arranged the invitations and television announcement to get even.

# This is a Raid

**B**efore his marriage to Sarah Ferguson in July 1986, Prince Andrew held a party for some of his friends. Towards the end of the evening three policewomen entered the club, stayed for a short while and then left it. It turned out that they were Pamela Stevenson, Princess Di and Sarah Ferguson!

# Prince Charles' Practical Joke

**I**n 1971 it was announced over the public address system at the RAF base at Cranwell, England, that a defect had been discovered in all the shoes that had been issued to officers. The owners were asked to hand in their shoes for

checking. A great many officers did so, but those that recognized the voice knew better. It was Prince Charles, who had a reputation for pulling practical jokes.

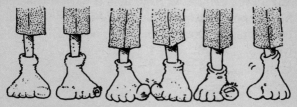

# Napoleon's Practical Joke

At a parade one day Napoleon Bonaparte presented one of his marshals with a beautiful baton. The marshal was extremely proud to receive such a handsome gift from the emperor. But his pride turned to horror when the baton began to bend! The baton was made of wax. Napoleon was making fun of the marshall, whom he considered much too pompous.

# Onassis' Practical Joke

The Greek millionaire, Aristotle Onassis, once paid for a whole page in a Paris newspaper to print a hoax reporting that the Eiffel Tower was to be loaned to Greece.

# Rudolph Valentino's Practical Joke

Heart-throb film star Rudolph Valentino apologized to the audience at a film première for appearing in his pajamas. He had overslept, he said. Then to everyone's surprise he began to take his pajamas off! The audience gasped, but soon started laughing. Valentino was wearing a full suit underneath.

# 3 · If You Believe This . . .

## The Invisible Fish

A pet shop in Surrey, England, displayed a large fish tank in its window, along with a sign advertising invisible Malayan ghost fish. Quite a crowd gathered outside the shop. The onlookers peered into the tank in the window, but saw no fish in it. Of course, the tank was empty, but would you believe that quite a few people actually went into the shop to ask the price of the non-existent fish?

# Sentences from the Sentenced

When an ad appeared in several European magazines stating that some young Italian girls were looking for male pen pals, many men replied. Several of them built up a regular correspondence and eventually arranged a meeting with the girls. Each exchange followed the same pattern. The girl would write to say that she did not have enough money to make the trip. In most cases, the man, who by then thought he had a good chance of marrying the girl, would send her the fare. But when he went to the meeting place, the girl did not show up.

One man decided to investigate further and went to visit the girl at her own home. When he got there, he found out that the address was a jail. The "young Italian girls" were in fact five male prisoners who made quite a bit of money from their scam.

# Turtle Trick

The Paris hotel manager was pleased when one of the hotel guests, Waldo Peirce, bought her a present. It was a small turtle, and she kept it in her room.

She looked after it so well that it grew at a rapid pace. Within a few days it had become enormous. But then a worrisome thing happened. The turtle began to get smaller. No matter how much she cared for it, it continued to get smaller and smaller every day.

Then she discovered that Waldo Peirce had tricked her. Each day, he had put a different-sized turtle in her room. What she had thought was one turtle getting bigger and then smaller was really a series of turtles all planted by Peirce.

# Please Destroy Your Telephone

The telephone caller claimed that he was a telephone engineer. "There's a rather serious fault," he said. "Your line is blocking all the other telephones in the area. Could you please cut the cord and that will free the congestion. There will be a telephone engineer at your house in 20 minutes to mend your phone."

Surprisingly, many people in Lancashire, England, who received that call believed it was genuine and dutifully cut the telephone cord as instructed. Real telephone engineers were not too pleased when they heard about the hoax. They had quite a few telephones to repair.

# Wet Phones

Maybe it was the same prankster who called people in north London saying he was an engineer and that there was a fault on the telephone

line that could only be fixed if the receiver was dunked in a bucket of water. Many people believed him. Real telephone engineers had quite a job repairing the wet phones.

## Stone's Stories

Louis T. Stone of Winsted, Connecticut, was a reporter with an unusual flair. He did not report stories—he made them up. Many of the newspaper editors who used his material between 1895 and 1933 knew the stories were hoaxes—but they were so popular they continued to print them.

Among Stone's stories was one about a bald man who was pestered by flies—so he painted a spider on his head to keep them away. Another told about a chicken farmer who plucked his chickens with a vacuum cleaner. And, there was one about a cat with a harelip that could whistle "Yankee Doodle Dandy."

Stone made the town of Winsted so famous that a sign was erected that said:

Winsted, Connecticut, founded in 1779, has been put on the map by the ingenious and queer stories that emanate from this town and which are printed all over the country, thanks to L.T. Stone.

## Grows Hair

In 1977 thousands of bald men invaded a farm in Northumberland, England, following a spoof television report announcing that water from the well had amazing hair-restoring properties.

# Men on the Moon

Now we know that there is no life on the moon, but years ago, many people believed that there was.

In 1835, one newspaper reported that the astronomer, Sir John Herschel, had discovered life on the moon. The paper said that Sir John was in South Africa testing a powerful new telescope. With this remarkable device he was able to see trees, vegetables, vegetation, oceans, beaches, buffaloes, goats and pelicans on the lunar surface.

Later it stated that the astronomer had seen people on the moon. They lived in caves and had long wings attached to their shoulders.

The stories convinced so many people that the *Journal of Commerce* asked permission to reproduce the articles in a scientific pamphlet. It was then that the truth was revealed.

Both the author, Richard Adams Locke, and the newspaper, the *New York Sun*, admitted that the stories were a hoax. It would certainly have had to have been quite a remarkable telescope to reveal all that!

# The Three-Humped Camel Prank

An ad in a local paper in Wales read: "Lost—one three-humped camel. Owner desperate. Reward." A telephone number was given for people to call.

The owner of a local shop was not pleased. It was his number that the prankster had listed. Over 70 people called him, claiming to have seen his three-humped camel.

## Hogging Attention

People in England flocked to fairs in the 19th century to see some amazing things on display. One famous exhibit was the pig-faced lady.

To gullible people of the time she appeared genuine enough. But the pig-faced lady was no lady. She was in reality a bear, with its face and paws shaved, dressed in women's clothing.

# Shaggy-Dog Story

A large number of talented animals have been featured on television. Possibly the most remarkable was a sheepdog called Tramp. Tramp was so clever he could even drive a car.

One program showed Tramp at the wheel of a small sports car, and he certainly was a very competent driver. Many viewers thought it was dangerous to let a dog drive a car, and hundreds telephoned in to complain. What they did not realize was that Tramp was really a woman dressed in a sheepdog costume.

# Cat Catch

One of the exhibits on display at one of P.T. Barnum's shows was the Cherry-Colored Cat. When visitors had paid their money, they were shown an ordinary black cat. Well, some cherries are black!

## Mark Twain's Cat

Sometimes a hoax can rebound on the hoaxer. This happened to the famous author, Mark Twain. He advertised in a newspaper that he had lost his cat, which was "so black that it could not be seen in ordinary light." Almost 1,000 people called at his house claiming that they had found his invisible cat!

## Charlie Chaplin—You Lose!

The great film comedian Charlie Chaplin once entered a Charlie Chaplin Look-Alike Contest for a laugh. To his surprise, he didn't win.

# 4 · Hush-Hush

## Whose Secret Weapon?

During World War II a new weapon called the Panjandrum was invented. It consisted of two 10-foot-high wheels joined by an axle. It had rocket charges around each wheel that were designed to propel it forward over land and sea.

The Panjandrum was built in absolute secrecy in England. Partway through its construction, workmen realized that the building in which it was being made was going to be too small to house it! They had to remove one wall of the shed so that construction could continue.

That wasn't the only blunder. The Panjandrum was tested on a beach in September 1943. When the machine was placed in the sea and the rockets were ignited, one of them fell off. The machine turned around and headed in the wrong direction.

A new test was arranged for the next day. This time the Panjandrum covered about 400 yards—twice as far as on the first test—before it got bogged down in the sand.

Adjustments were made and a third wheel, carrying more rockets, was added. This time the rockets wouldn't ignite.

During the months that followed, more adjustments were made and more tests were carried out. The final test came in January of 1944. High-ranking officers were invited to watch the amazing new secret weapon in action. Now everything went wrong! Some rockets fell off, and the Panjandrum went wildly out of control. Before long it headed towards the officers who had come to

watch, and they had to run for their lives! Then it turned and headed out to sea where it disintegrated completely.

After that the project was abandoned.

## Soft Landing

It was no real surprise to the British hydroplane crew that the air vice-marshal wanted to inspect their craft. (Hydroplanes, in use during the first half of the 20th Century, were aircraft that took off from and landed only on water.) After

takeoff, the air vice-marshal asked if he could take the controls. Everything went well until the air vice-marshal prepared to land. The crew looked down in horror—they were heading straight for an airfield runway! As politely as he could under the circumstances, one of the crew members reminded the air vice-marshal that an airfield landing would not be appropriate.

The air vice-marshal took the hint and headed back towards a stretch of water where he touched

down. He thanked the crewman for reminding him that he was flying a hydroplane—and then he opened the door and calmly stepped out!

## Could the RAF Be Wrong?

An RAF airman was surprised to receive notice that he was going to be discharged from the

service. He was even more surprised when he read the reason—he was pregnant! The computer had made an error.

## Monty's Double

During World War II Field Marshal Montgomery seemed to have the ability to be in two places at once. Actually, he *was* in two places at once. Some of Monty's appearances were not him at all, but an actor who looked and sounded like him.

## The Brilliant Death of Willy Martin

In 1943, during the Second World War, the body of Major William Martin was discovered off a Spanish beach. He was buried with full military honors at Huelva in southwest Spain.

Documents he had been carrying were returned to London where they were carefully examined. It

was obvious that they had been tampered with, and that was exactly what the British had hoped would happen: for Major Martin was a hoax designed to fool the Germans.

Willy Martin did not exist. The body was that of a man who had died of pneumonia, a death that would be consistent with death by drowning if the

body were recovered from the sea. With the permission of the man's parents, the body had been put into the sea near Spain in the hope that the Germans would find it and read the fake papers it carried. The papers stated that the Allies would attack Sardinia, when in fact they intended to attack Sicily.

The hoax was an immense success. When the Allies launched their offensive, most of the heavy German equipment had been moved to defend the island of Sardinia.

You can see an excellent film based upon this

incident, called *The Man Who Never Was*. It starred Clifton Webb as the mastermind of the plan, Gloria Grahame as a girl who unwittingly played the role of Willy Martin's fiancée, and Stephen Boyd, as the clever spy sent by the Germans to check out the authenticity of Willy Martin.

## Explosion in Rome

When he arrived in New York after a flight from Rome on October 2, 1985, General James Brown found a telegram waiting for him. It was from the police in Rome, telling him that they had blown up his car.

When the general made inquiries, he found the telegram to be authentic. The chauffeur who had driven the general to the Rome airport had parked

the car near the ticket office of a foreign airline. Police, always on the lookout for terrorists, believed that the car might contain a bomb. Then they discovered that the license plate of the car was a phony and they feared the worst. So they had the car blown up.

Apparently, the false license plates had been put on the car for security purposes—but no one on the general's staff had thought of informing the local police!

## Is This Any Way to Run a War?

President Lyndon Johnson once visited an air base to improve the morale of troops who were going to be sent to fight in Vietnam. But the morale of the troops he was scheduled to meet was so low (and they had had so much to drink) that their officers didn't think they were fit to be seen.

Their solution was to allow the President to meet troops who had just *returned* from Vietnam. Those men were very excited to be back that they were laughing and joking. The President was so impressed that he insisted on waving goodbye to them as their plane took off. Of course, the men were not going anywhere—they had just come home.

The men had to get back on the plane from which they had just disembarked and perform a fake departure. The aircraft then flew around the base until the President left.

It Appeared in the *Manchester Guardian*:

## Iron Lady

What Mrs. Thatcher's closest friends are wondering is whether, as the signs suggest, she is beginning to suffer from metal fatigue.

# 5 · April Fool

## Who's Zoo?

**Z**oos around the world dread April Fools' Day. On that day each year they are certain to receive calls from Mr. L.E. Phant, Mr. C. Lyon, Mrs. G. Raffe and Mr. Albert Ross.

# The Bare-Fronted Hoodwink

In the Royal Scottish Museum in Edinburgh there is a strange-looking bird. It has a large black head, brown wings and a white breast with a large patch of bright red.

The bird was first shown on April 1, 1975, and the date gives a clue to its origins. It was "made" by Willie Sterling, a taxidermist at the museum. He named the bird "the bare-fronted hoodwink."

# A Boost for the Museum

In 1960, the directors of the Gothenburg Museum in Sweden were looking for a way to attract more visitors to their displays. They decided to exhibit a strange creature called a *Vitrysk Strandmuddlare* (a white Russian shore-muddler).

Asked for a description, the museum reported

that the white Russian shore-muddler is a very strange creature. Its head and front legs are like a baby wild pig, its tusks are like the teeth of an alligator, its hindquarters and tail are similar to those of a squirrel and its back feet are like those of a water fowl.

The *Vitrysk Strandmuddlare* was such a deliberate hoax that it's unlikely that anyone would be fooled into believing it was real. But just in case, the museum displays the creature only once a year—on April 1.

# The Green Cliffs of Dover

Listeners to BBC Radio Four's "Today" program were once told on April 1 that fast-breeding algae were turning the white cliffs of Dover green. Many listeners believed it.

# Spaghetti Harvest

On April 1, 1957, a film about the Swiss spaghetti harvest was shown on British television. It was narrated by Richard Dimbleby, one of the country's most respected commentators. Swiss peasants were shown gathering spaghetti from the trees in the Ticino district, and Dimbleby gave a serious explanation of how spring had come early that year, producing a bumper spaghetti harvest.

Hundreds of people telephoned the BBC after the program. There were no complaints that they had been hoaxed—all they wanted to know was where they could buy spaghetti plants. In answer to this question they were told that such plants were not available in England but that some U.S. enthusiasts had achieved interesting results by planting a small can of spaghetti in tomato sauce!

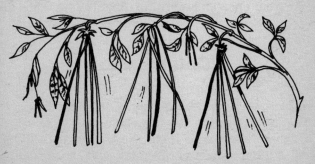

# Which Side Are They On?

An April Fools' item on Paris radio once caused traffic chaos in the French capital. It was announced that from April 1 all Europe would drive on the left.

The result was pandemonium: Some drivers who had heard the broadcast actually believed it and drove on the left side of the road. Of course, those who had not listened stayed on the right, but they had no idea what was going on. No fatalities were reported.

# Color Radio

Everyone knows the world is full of modern scientific wonders, so it was no surprise to some English listeners to Radio Norwich that their local station was experimenting with color radio.

This new system, listeners were warned, would alter the brilliance of tuning lights on their radios.

Listeners commented that the experiment seemed fairly successful, but they had some problems with it. One of them complained that colors were flashing from his radio. Another moaned that the experiment was affecting traffic lights in his area. This was quite a surprise to the broadcasters who had transmitted the item as an April Fools' joke!

## How to Defy Gravity

Patrick Moore is a respected astronomer with a great reputation as an expert in his field. One morning in 1976 he explained on a BBC radio program that the gravitational pull on Earth would be decreased by the fact that the planet Pluto was

passing close to Jupiter. To test it, he told people to jump into the air at exactly 9:47 that morning. They would feel lighter, he said, and would be able to float in the air for several seconds.

It seems that lots of people believed him, because they telephoned the BBC to say that the experiment had worked. They must have been very gullible, particularly since the date was April 1!

## Wrong Flight

A group of businessmen flying to Belfast, Ireland, on April 1, 1980, were surprised to hear the announcement, "We shall shortly be arriving in Paris." Some of them may have hoped it was true—but it turned out to be another April Fools' prank.

# 6 · Great Practical Jokers

## A Cheep Trick

During World War II, British Prime Minister Winston Churchill often had meetings with President Franklin Delano Roosevelt. The two men sometimes ate breakfast together while discussing world affairs. One day Churchill received quite a surprise. He cracked open his boiled egg—and a live chick popped out!

Churchill had fallen prey to Roosevelt's favorite joke. Before breakfast F.D.R. had put the chick into an empty shell, made some pinholes in part of the shell so that the chick could breathe, and then sealed the two halves together.

# Footprints on the Ceiling

Aman was visiting his friend, President Abraham Lincoln, when he received quite a surprise. Entering one of the rooms, he saw that someone had walked across the ceiling! Up the walls and across the ceiling there was a track of clear footprints.

Later he discovered that Lincoln was the man behind the hoax. It was one of his favorite jokes. He would have a room painted and then hold someone upside down while he "walked" across the ceiling, leaving footprints in the paint.

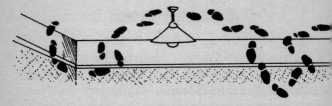

# Money in the Streets

There in the middle of the sidewalk on a London street was a genuine 5-pound note. Sooner or later someone was bound to notice it and pick it up. But the person who did so was in for a surprise. The note was glued to the pavement. What the victim did not see was Horace d

Vere Cole watching and laughing in the background. In the 1920s Cole was known as the greatest practical joker of all time and this was one of his favorite pranks.

# An Arresting Prank

The British politician, Oliver Locker-Lampson, once announced that it was unthinkable that anyone would ever arrest an MP (Member of Parliament). But he didn't figure on the tricks of Horace de Vere Cole, who was quick to prove him wrong.

Cole challenged the politician to a race along a London street, and Locker-Lampson accepted. As he explained the rules of the race, Cole secretly slipped his watch into the MP's pocket.

Then they were off and running. Cole let Locker-Lampson build up a good lead. Then he

followed, shouting, "Stop, thief!" The police joined in the chase, and when the "stolen" watch was discovered in Locker-Lampson's pocket, the unfortunate politician was arrested.

Once the arrest was made Cole revealed the hoax—too bad for him—because he, too, was arrested! Eventually, however, both men were released, but Cole had made his point.

## Horace Strikes Again

"**E**xcuse me, sir," said a surveyor to a person in the street. "I am a surveyor and I wonder if you could please help me by holding this tape measure for a second or two."

In most cases, the stranger would agree. And then the surveyor, who was actually Horace de Vere Cole, would go around the corner and ask another person to hold the other end of the tape.

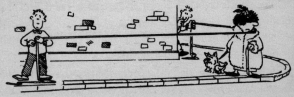

Cole would then retire to a nearby shop doorway and wait, tears of laughter running down his cheeks, for the moment when his two victims realized that they had been hoaxed.

## An Amusing Feet

When American prankster Hugh Troy was at Cornell University in Ithaca, New York, he played a joke on one of his professors. He painted human feet on the tops of the professor's boots and then painted over them with black paint so that the boots appeared normal. But the black paint wasn't waterproof, and when the professor walked out in the rain, it dissolved, leaving him apparently walking about in his bare feet!

## The "Big Red" Rhinoceros

On a snowy day at Cornell "Big Red" University, Hugh Troy borrowed a friend's waste-

paper basket that was made from the foot of a rhinoceros. He tied some lengths of rope to it and then, with the help of a friend swung the foot back and forth so that it left footprints in the snow. Keeping some distance away from the prints they were making, the two men walked through the university campus.

The next day, the footprints were identified by a zoologist as those of a rhinoceros! The event caused quite a stir—especially since the prints ended in the middle of the frozen lake in the middle of which was an enormous hole!

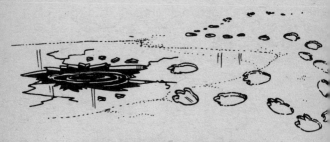

# What's Been Stolen?

**H**ugh Troy once left a pile of burglary equipment outside New York's Metropolitan Museum of Art. This caused a stir among the museum staff. They organized a frantic search of the premises to see which of their treasures had been stolen during the night.

## Dig We Must

A road crew was repairing a Manhattan street when an official from the head office appeared. He told the crew to go to another site, a short distance away, and dig there. When they had dug a good size hole, the official left. It was only then, when traffic was in chaos all around them, that the workmen realized they had been fooled. The "man from the head office" turned out to be famous prankster Hugh Troy.

## Some People Will Steal Anything...

A policeman, walking through Central Park in New York, saw a man running off with one of the park benches. He caught him and arrested him, but the man then produced a receipt for the bench. It belonged to him! The man was arch

joker Hugh Troy, and he had bought the bench a short while earlier with the sole intention of hoaxing a policeman.

## Air Shortage

Overweight Americans were alarmed when it was announced that anyone weighing over 195 pounds was to be deported. This drastic measure had become necessary, newspaper reports said, because pollution was leading to a shortage of oxygen. As fat people consumed more than their fair share of air, they had to go.

People realized that the proposal was a hoax when they discovered that the reports had been written by Alan Abel, who was well known for his amazing and successful practical jokes.

## Animals Should Be Clothed

On May 27, 1959, G. Clifford Prout, President of the Society Against Indecency of Naked Animals, appeared on TV insisting that all animals should be clothed. He claimed that moral

standards in America were declining due to the fact that animals were allowed to go around naked.

The broadcast was an immediate success and thousands of letters and postcards arrived at the Society's headquarters promising their support. Numerous other television, radio, and newspaper interviews followed.

The Society's campaign to rid the world of naked animals continued for six years—and fooled many people. The Society was another invention of New York's principal prankster, Alan Abel.

## Vote for Yetta

New York's Yetta Bronstein was one of the candidates in the 1964 American Presidential campaign. Her slogan was "Vote for Yetta and

things will get better." Yetta Bronstein was a middle-aged housewife from the Bronx who felt that the country needed a mother figure. It seemed a lot of ordinary voters agreed with her: "I'm voting for Yetta" badges were worn all over the city.

No one seemed to wonder why Yetta Bronstein was never seen in public or why there were no photographs of her. The reason was simple—she did not exist! She had been invented by Alan Abel and his wife.

# 7 · Whose Idea Was That?

## Fingerprint Burn

Gangster John Dillinger knew his fingerprints were on file with the FBI. He thought it would be a good idea if he got some new fingerprints, so he put the tips of his thumbs and fingers in acid to remove his old prints. He endured weeks of agony until his skin healed. But when he compared his new fingerprints with his old ones, they were exactly the same!

# All at Sea

Sir Henry Bessemer, famous for inventing a new steel-making process, always felt seasick when he traveled by ship, so he designed a ship that he thought would not make people feel ill. He

decided that the center of the vessel should swing independently from the rest of the ship. Then, when the ship rolled in heavy seas, he figured the center portion would remain level and the passengers would not feel the vessel's motion.

A steamer of this design was built and called the *Bessemer* but, when it was tested, the center portion rolled *more* than an ordinary vessel! Sir Henry then added a hydraulic brake to be operated by a man who sat watching a spirit level that was linked to the center portion of the ship. Every time the ship rolled, the man would apply the brake just enough to keep the center level. This proved even worse than before! As a result, the center portion was fixed, and the vessel was used as a regular ship.

But the vessel's problems were far from over. It was almost unsteerable. On its first trip it crashed into the pier at Calais. It then returned to Dover and hit the pier there. At last, the *Bessemer* was withdrawn from service.

## Eggs-plosion

**P**olice officer Kevin Doherty was having a boiled egg during his coffee break early one morning in December, 1985. As he dipped his spoon into the egg a terrific explosion rocked the tiny canteen in Lancashire, England. At first, he and his friends thought they were the victims of a terrorist attack, but it turned out that the blast was the result of a basic blunder by officer Doherty. He had boiled his egg, but deciding that

it was undercooked, he put it in the microwave oven for a few seconds and then tried it again.

Now, one thing that should never be cooked in a microwave is an egg in its shell, even if the top has been taken off. Enormous pressure builds up inside the egg. It was the release of this pressure when the policeman pushed his spoon into the egg that caused the explosion.

## Crash, Bang, Wallop

Romark was a successful hypnotist and mind reader who had his own TV series. On October 12, 1977, he prepared to perform a psychic feat for which he had become famous. Two coins were placed over his eyes, covered with dough, and held in place by thick bandages tied around his head. It was impossible for him to see anything, but Romark was confident that his incredible powers would enable him to drive a car through the streets of Ilford, in Essex, while

blindfolded. He got into a yellow Renault and pro-
ceeded down Cranbrook Road. Seconds later his
confidence and his reputation were shattered. He
crashed—straight into the back of a parked police
car!

## Cruelest Cut

When people complained about the overgrown
garden in Akron, Ohio, the town council
sent some of their men to cut down the weeds. It
proved to be an expensive error, because a judge
later ordered the council to pay $1,500 worth of
compensation to the householder. He was a vege-
tarian and had been growing weeds to eat.

# High Flyer

It seemed a good idea at the time. Larry Walters tied 42 gas balloons to a deck chair and then took off. The system worked better than he had expected. Within minutes, he was flying three miles high—and still climbing. It gave pilots from the nearby airport, at Long Beach, California quite a shock. They reported a strange man flying in a deck chair.

Larry was eventually able to land after bursting some of the balloons with his penknife. But when he landed he was immediately arrested for flying without a license!

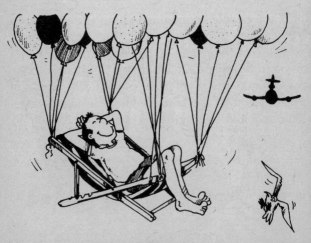

# Dirty Work

Contractors were asked by the council of Penistone, near Sheffield, England, to clean the stonework on 50 houses. But the council forgot to inform one of the householders, Mrs. Robinson. When she first saw the workmen, they had already cleaned the lower half of her house, Mrs. Robinson said, "It's taken 35 years to give this house character. I want it to stay dirty." The contractors offered to clean the rest of the house for nothing, but Mrs. Robinson insisted that the men put the dirt back on to the house! They did!

# Power Cut

Town councils always try to save money where they can. But sometimes they are not successful. This was certainly the case in 1974 when the town council in one village switched off the street lights for three days, as a money-saver.

They saved about $20.84. Later, they discovered that it had cost $33.26 to switch the electricity off and an additional $21 for putting it back on again. Instead of saving money the "economy measure" had added $33.42 to the council's costs!

# The Car That Was No-go

For a long time, General Motors had been having trouble selling their Chevy Nova in South America. At last someone pointed out that "No-va" in colloquial Spanish means "won't go."

# 8 · Crime Really Doesn't Pay

## Remember to Lock Up Before You Go

Three bandits who held up a Colorado bank proved quite successful. When they had collected enough money, they shut the bank staff in the vault, thinking that would give them time to get away. But they made one vital mistake—they forgot to lock the vault. The bank staff walked right out and raised the alarm. The thieves were caught soon after.

# This is a Zip-Up

**R**obber Raymond Burles walked into a Paris bank, brandishing a gun, and ordered the cashiers to put money in his bag. Then he zipped up the bag and ordered everyone to stay where they were as he backed out of the bank. But no one paid any attention to what he said. Instead of standing still with their hands up, they jumped on him and called the police. Why were the people in the bank no longer afraid of him? He had zipped up the gun in the bag along with the money—by mistake.

# Armed Robber

**A**n armed masked man who robbed a bank in Kentucky might have gotten away with it, except that he made a similar mistake. It was a hot day, and he had rolled up his sleeves, forgetting he had a tattoo on his arm—with his name on it!

# Hat Trick

A gunman who robbed a Paris grocery store thought he had made a clean getaway. But as he ran, his hat blew off. It was not long before the police caught up with him—his name and address were inside the hat.

# Be Prepared

A bank robber went up to the cashier of an Oregon bank and pushed a note across the counter. It read: "This is a holdup and I've got a gun. Put all the money in a paper bag."

The cashier read the note and then wrote on it, "I don't have a paper bag." The confused robber fled as quickly as he could, probably vowing to bring a bag with him next time.

# In the Dark

**A**rt Eastman waited until everyone had left the shop before he went in to rob the owner. He took out a gun, pulled down his homemade mask and charged into the shop. But he had overlooked one thing; when planning the robbery, he had forgotten to put eyeholes in the mask, and he couldn't see a thing. As he stumbled around in the dark, he pushed up his mask to see where he was. Later the shopkeeper was able to give police a perfect description of him.

# Letter Catch

**W**hen gunman, William Lindley, robbed a Georgia bank, he also goofed badly. The note he handed the cashier was written on an envelope—and the envelope had his name and address on it!

# Swallow That!

Con man Peter Lazardes thought he had a good idea. He stole some diamonds and then swallowed them. When it was discovered that the stones were missing, no one thought of X-raying Lazardes. But he did not get away with the crime. The stones were discovered, still lodged in his stomach, when he died six months later.

# Bad Day for Bandits

It was a bad day for the bandits who tried to rob a factory safe in Staffordshire, England, in November 1979. First they tried to break into the safe without realizing that it was not even locked. Then they failed to turn on the oxygen on their cutting equipment so that the hot acetylene flame did not cut but simply melted a hole in the front of the safe. Finally, one of the robbers put his hand through the hole but could not find any money—the safe was empty!

# Photo Fit

**D**uring a raid on a house in the north of England, two burglars found a camera. Just for a laugh, they took photographs of themselves. But they dropped the camera as they were making their getaway from the house. When the film was later developed, it didn't take the police long to find them.

# Handy Cover-Up

**A**nother burglar thought he had a good idea. He took his socks off and wore them on his hands so he wouldn't leave any fingerprints. But police in Chattanooga, Tennessee arrested him soon after. They identified him by his footprints!

## Slippery Customer

When the thief in Sheffield, England, saw an upstairs window of a house slightly ajar, he thought he was onto a good thing. He shinnied up the drainpipe and slipped inside. The room was occupied by a 13-foot boa constrictor. The thief quickly backed out of the window, forgetting he was upstairs. He ended up with a broken leg.

## Say "Cheese"

The two thieves, charged with robbing a golf clubhouse, were surprised when police offered them each a piece of cheese. It was to lead to their downfall, for their toothmarks exactly matched those found in a piece of cheese left in the golf clubhouse.

# Thief Who Talked Too Much

**D**uring a burglary in 1980, robber John Yianni narrowly escaped being caught. Afterwards, he telephoned his apartment, where a friend was waiting to hear from him. He described what had happened. "Why don't you come round and tell me more about it?" said his friend. Yianni went home and was promptly arrested. It was not his friend to whom he had been talking. It was the police.

## Between You and Me . . .

**T**wo criminals who made a dash for freedom from an English court in 1985 made just one mistake. They forgot they were handcuffed together and when they came to a lamp post, one ran to the right side and the other to the left! The police had no trouble recapturing the stunned pair.

# Bungled Burglary

The robbers had planned the supermarket burglary in Navan, Ireland, down to the last detail. They would enter an attic at the rear of the building, make a hole in the floor and climb down into the supermarket.

Getting into the attic was fairly easy, but when they started to dig a hole in the attic floor, it was harder than they had expected. It turned out to be made of reinforced concrete and it took several hours to break through. At long last, the hole was finished and the robbers jumped through—to find themselves outside. They had miscalculated the length of the store.

# Food for Thought

Three masked robbers were lying in wait in a supermarket parking lot in New York, when Howard Selley and Wilfred Parsons, two employees of the store came out carrying a plastic

bag. The robbers put on their masks, pointed their guns and demanded that the men hand over the morning's receipts.

The two men were surprised, but willingly handed over the bag. The robbers were even more surprised when they looked inside the bag. It contained apples and cheese sandwiches, which the two men had been planning to have for a midday snack.

## Train Trap

A burglar had just finished robbing a department store in Hamburg, West Germany, when he spotted a model train set. He was still playing with it three hours later when the police arrived!

## Too Good To Be True

Another West German crook found that it doesn't pay to be too good at your job. He figured out a way to make counterfeit coins, but the

...nes he produced were more perfect than real 5-...nark coins even were. It was not long before he ...as apprehended.

## An Arresting Party

Over 100 people made a big mistake on December 16, 1985, when they accepted an invitation to a party in Washington, D.C. Supposedly, the party had been arranged by a sports promotion firm, but what the partygoers—all of them wanted by the police—did not know was that the "sports firm" did not exist. All the people in fancy dress at the party were police officers. The "guests" soon found out, however, what the purpose of the party really was when the host made the announcement, "We have a special surprise for you. You are under arrest. Put your hands up."

# Language Barrier

A Scotsman bought a toy gun and went into a stationery store in Luton, England. He pointed the gun at a salesgirl and said, "This is a stickup." But because of his broad Scottish accent, the girl could not understand a word.

"Bang, bang," said the would-be robber. "You're dead," replied the girl, and she burst into fits of laughter. The robber felt he had no alternative but to leave empty-handed.

# 9 · Most Embarrassing Moments

## Most Embarrassing Air Strike

During Peruvian Air Force Week in 1975, 30 fighter planes took part in a demonstration of skill. Fourteen old fishing boats were towed out to sea and the Peruvian air force flew in for the attack. For the next 15 minutes the target vessels were bombed and strafed to the delight of the watching crowd. But at the end of the display, the admiration of the onlookers turned to amazement. Not one of the 14 vessels had been hit!

## Most Embarrassing Art Award

The American Academy of Design was so impressed by a painting submitted by Edward Dickenson that they gave him a top art award. They were rather embarrassed to discover that they had conducted their judging with the painting hanging upside down!

## Most Embarrassing Award Presentation

On February 13, 1979, architects met on Skegness Pier on the northeast coast of England to present George Sunderland with an award for the best-designed pier theatre.

During the presentation ceremony, the theatre was swept out to sea.

# Most Embarrassing Fire Alarm

Caroline McKenna was working in the Ship Inn, Wokingham, in southern England, when two firemen rushed in and asked to use the telephone. They called the fire department to come out urgently—the fire engine was on fire!

# Most Embarrassing Anniversary Event

To mark the 40th anniversary of the United Nations in 1985, it was decided to ask climbers to scale Mount Everest and plant a UN flag on the summit. But the expedition ended in disaster. Unfortunately for the climbers, they picked a time when the weather was the worst it had been for many years. Although they managed to brave the cold and the incessant winds, they were forced to abandon the climb 800 feet from the summit. Getting even that far was quite a remarkable achievement—but the climbers slipped up

when they planted the flag and took the photograph that was supposed to appear all over the world. The flag was upside down!

# Most Embarrassing Wrong Purchase

Someone slipped up in Clairton, Pennsylvania, when it was decided to buy a sleek 43-foot-long fire engine for the town. The engine was so long it could not be used on most of the town's narrow streets. Embarrassed town officials had to return it in exchange for two smaller models.

# Most Embarrassing Museum Mistake

One of the exhibits in a museum in South Shields, England, was a Roman coin said to be dated between 135 and 138 A.D. But nine-year-old Fiona Gordon was not impressed. On seeing the coin she said it was nothing but a plastic

token. Museum officials were amused by the young girl. But when they checked again they found that she was right. The coin bore a Roman-style design but it was definitely made of plastic. The letter R on the coin, which experts had taken to mean "Rome," was in fact the initial letter of a soft-drink manufacturer!

It Appeared in the Middlesbrough
Evening Gazette:

## Nosey

The attempt at burglary backfired when security guards heard the nose of a fruit machine being forced.

# Most Embarrassing Weather Forecast

John Nash, an amateur weather forecaster, predicted that the city of Adelaide, Australia, would be hit by a tidal wave. He was so sure of this forecast that he moved from Adelaide to a town called Warwick, which he said was the safest place in Australia. A month later, there was heavy flooding—in Warwick.

# Most Embarrassing Tug-of-War Tournament

Eight teams turned up for a tug-of-war in northern England. But the match had to be cancelled—the organizers forgot to bring a rope!

# Most Embarrassing Treaty

The agreement to end World War I was signed in November 1918. But those who signed it did not notice, until afterwards, the mistake made by the person who had typed it. The typist had put some of the sheets of carbon paper into the typewriter the wrong way. As a result, some sections of this historic document could only be read backwards!

# Most Embarrassing Dance

Nancy Reagan, wife of President Ronald Reagan, thought she had planned everything down to the last detail for the Queen of England's visit to the White House in 1980. But she blundered on one important point—the music for the

Queen's dance with the President. As the Queen and the President moved onto the dance floor, the band played, "The Lady is a Tramp."

## Most Embarrassing Bank Robbery

**W**ould-be bank robber Carlo Colondi really slipped up when he tried to rob a bank in Milan, Italy. As he burst through the door he tripped on the doormat, his scarf fell from his face and his gun went off—though it didn't hurt anyone.

When he got up and headed for the cashier, he slipped and fell over again on the floor.

Confused by the laughter of the customers and staff, Colondi rushed out to his car. There he was arrested—he'd left his car in a no-parking area.

## Most Embarrassing Train Ride

**A**s the train conductor approached, Edward Nye told his friend, poet James Whitcomb Riley, to get under the seat because he only had one ticket. Riley was reluctant to follow his friend's request, but eventually did so to avoid any trouble.

When the inspector reached him, Nye handed over two tickets. "Who's the other ticket for?" asked the inspector. Nye pointed to Riley, half hidden beneath the seat. "It's for my friend," Nye said. "He always travels like that!"

# Most Embarrassing Locked Car

One cold day in 1979, Peter Rowlands tried to open his car door but couldn't because the lock was frozen. He decided that the best way to defrost the lock was to breathe into it. He placed his mouth against the lock and blew. When he tried to get up, he found to his horror that his lips had frozen to the car! He remained stuck for 20 minutes.

# 10 · Show Biz Goofs

## Another Charioteer

**M**any blunders are made in filmmaking and lots of mistakes actually appear in finished films.

In the film, *Ben Hur*, that takes place in ancient Rome, there is a magnificent chariot race. But somebody goofed, for in that scene—if you're sharp—you can see a little red sports car passing by in the distance.

# The Magic Earring

It is very easy to let mistakes get by when making a film. In one scene in *The King and I*, for example, Yul Brynner, who plays the king, is seen wearing an earring in some shots. In others the earring has mysteriously disappeared!

# On Reflection

One of the most obvious film goofs appear in the 1954 film, *Carmen Jones*. In one shot the camera followed the heroine along a street, but nobody noticed, until the film was released, that a reflection of the camera was visible in every shop window.

## Very Early Television

The film, *The Wrong Box*, is an amusing comedy set in Victorian times (the end of the 19th century). But one of the jokes was completely unintentional. The filmmakers forgot that television was not invented until 1926, and they allowed television antennas to appear clearly on the rooftops.

## Repeat Showing

On December 31, 1986, millions of West Germans sat down to watch their president's New Year speech on television. When Herr von Weizsaecker began talking, many viewers thought that the speech had a familiar ring to it. Those with good memories soon realized that the President was saying exactly the same thing that he had said the year before.

Later that evening, television chiefs apologized

for their error. It seems that engineers had put on the previous year's taped speech by mistake.

**It Appeared in the *Daily Express*:**

## Behind the Scenes

The Oliviers make one of their rear appearances together on British television.

## What Did I Say My Name Was?

Broadcasters quite often mess up their lines, but one English commentator got his own name wrong. He finished a news bulletin by saying: "This is *The World at One* with William Whitelaw." The only problem was that his name was Bill Hardcastle. William Whitelaw was then the Home Secretary of Great Britain.

# Opera Hang-Up

In 1956, opera singer Hans Hotter strode on to the stage of the Royal Opera House, London, during Act Three of *Die Walküre*. He was greeted by roars of laughter. He had been in such a rush to put on his cloak, he had not noticed that the coat hanger was sticking out of his collar!

# Music World's Biggest Mistake?

When the Decca record company first listened to a group called "The Beatles," their company executive Dick Rowe didn't like their sound. "Groups with guitars are on the way out," he said.

Other major record companies also rejected the group. They were eventually taken on by a small

record company, Parlophone, and went on to be the biggest stars the pop world has ever known.

## Hospital Howler

A disc jockey working for a trial period with the BBC dedicated one number to a listener who was in the hospital. He then said, "I think it would be nice to play this record for everyone who is in hospital at the moment. I hope it cheers you up." Unfortunately, the record that was played next was called, *"When I'm Dead and Gone."*

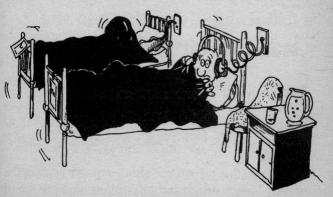

# Birthday Blunder

Tony Blackburn, the British disc jockey, once played a record for a man who was celebrating his 70th birthday. Blackburn never checked to see what the next record was. It was *"Knockin' On Heaven's Door."*

# Lost Results

A BBC commentator, presenting the sports report, was heard to say, "Nowhere are the football results."

There was an embarrassed silence and then he spoke again: "I'm sorry, I'll read that again. Now here are the football results."

# Gaining Something in the Translation

Executives of the Pepsi-Cola company thought they would do well in Germany with their famous advertising phrase, "Come alive with Pepsi." But they nearly slipped up. The translation into German read, "Come out of the grave with Pepsi."

# 11 · Sorry About That. . . .

## Wrestler who Beat Himself

A U.S. wrestler, Stanley Pinto, got tangled up in the ropes during one of his bouts. In his attempts to get free, he touched his shoulders to the mat for three seconds—and was declared the loser. His opponent was nowhere near him at the time!

# Death Wish

When newspapers mistakenly carried his obituary, writer Mark Twain said, "Reports of my death have been greatly exaggerated."

A similar thing happened to a man in Scotland. A report in the *Aberdeen Evening Express* said: "It is with regret we learn of the sudden death of Donald Everett, of Durris, and wish him an early return to full health."

# Grave Mistake

The funeral of 56-year-old Antonio Percelli at Palermo in Sicily went according to plan. The funeral directors had his grave all prepared for him. But then, without warning, he climbed out of his coffin. The efforts of the funeral directors were

not wasted, however. The shock of Antonio stepping out of his grave caused his mother-in-law to have a heart attack. So she was buried in the grave instead of him.

## It Got Hotter for Barton

Farmer Anton Barton in South Carolina got so hot while plowing his field that he stopped for a refreshing drink of beer. It was so tasty, he continued drinking during the rest of the day. After work he set off home. Unfortunately, all that beer had made him rather forgetful and he never raised the plow. By the time police caught up with him, he had plowed up two miles of roadway.

## Adventures of 911

When police in Humberside, England answered an emergency call in September 1985, they could hear moaning and groaning on the line. They asked the caller to give a name, but

obviously he or she wasn't able to do so. Telephone engineers traced the call to a house in Bridlington, but when police arrived there it was locked.

They traced the owner, Nick Clarke, at work and he rushed home. He expected to find is wife ill or injured. When he entered the house, however, his anguish turned to embarrassment. Domino, his dog, greeted him as he entered. In the dog's mouth was what was left of the telephone receiver! While chewing it the puppy had accidentally dialed emergency services.

## The No-Stop Stop

David Lashbrooke and his friend, John Henderson, were waiting for a train at a small station near Southampton, England, one Sunday in January, 1983. The train arrived and the boys

were about to get on, when the conductor put his head out of the window and stopped them.

"You can't get on," he said. "We don't stop here on Sundays."

"But you've stopped," David said, preparing to board.

"No, we only stopped to tell you we don't stop," said the conductor, as the train took off.

## Nothing Stops the Post Office

The British Post Office prides itself on the fact that most of its postal deliveries are made quickly. But sometimes they slip up—as they did with a postcard sent to Mrs. Marjorie Witts of Swansea in Wales in 1922. The postman delivered it in June, 1986—64 years late! The letter never did find Mrs. Witts. She had moved from that address 50 years before.

*Sorry About That . . . .* 99

# What's Wrong with This Sentence?

A magazine writer slipped up when he wrote: "If you asked six friends to name the commonest bird, the odds are that nine out of ten would say the sparrow."

**It Appeared in the _Essex County Standard_:**

## Obituary Notice

Greenwold, Florence May.—Late of 163 Bergholt Road, Colchester. A simple, kind, and loving old lady who died with great dignity at "Ambleside," Wood Lane, Fordham Heath, Colchester on Saturday, April 3, 1982 at 3:10 p.m. Loved by family and friends who knew her will.

# The Fish Won

Two hundred ambulance drivers lined up along the banks of a canal in Kidderminster, England, to take part in the annual angling championship. After five hours, no one had caught a fish. Someone had forgotten to tell the organizer that the fish had been removed to another location three weeks earlier.

# 12 · The Wrong Place at the Wrong Time

## The Great Escape

Fifty prisoners in a Mexican jail decided to escape. They planned everything down to the last detail and then began digging an escape tunnel. When the tunnel was finished, they scrambled down into it and came up in the courtroom where they had been sentenced!

# The Tooth of the Matter

When he escaped from Nevada State Prison, convict Clive Castro believed he had thought of everything. But he had forgotten one detail—he had left his false teeth behind in prison. After three days of freedom he was desperate for a steak, but without any teeth there was no way he could eat it. As far as he could see, there was only one thing to do—he gave himself up so that he could get back to his teeth.

# Escape to Prison

In June 1982, Thomas Gee had completed only two months of his 12-month prison sentence. He did not like the idea of spending another ten months behind bars, so he decided to escape. He was working in the prison's vegetable store when

he saw his chance. A truck arrived with a delivery of vegetables and Thomas quickly ducked under it and held on to part of the chassis.

When he had completed his delivery at the prison, the driver set off to his next stop. Little did he know that he was carrying a passenger! Thomas clung to the chassis for some time until the truck eventually slowed down and stopped. Covered in oil, he slipped from his hiding place—and was met by two prison officers. The truck's second delivery was at another jail—Thomas had escaped from one prison to another!

## He Did Time

A West German shoplifter shinnied down a drainpipe to escape police. He then climbed over a high wall and leaped into the yard below. Unfortunately, it was the yard of Dusseldorf Jail. Guards found stolen watches in his pockets. He ended up doing time.

## Hi, There!

D uring a bout of particularly cold weather in January 1987, a woman drove along an icy road in Chester, England, looking for Canal Street. Several people waved at her as she passed. She thought they were just being friendly, until

she realized they were trying to tell her something. She was driving on the frozen surface of the Shropshire Union Canal! She leaped out of her car and ran to the bank, just in time to see the vehicle sink through the ice into eight feet of water.

## Snow Joke

Heavy snow is not uncommon in New York, but in one blizzard, motorists got more than they bargained for. Because the snow was so deep, they were forced to abandon their cars. When they returned later to dig them out, they found they had parking tickets attached to their windshields!

## Longest Hospital Visit

In 1953 Mrs. Alice Coe went to visit her aunt in a mental hospital in Jamestown, Virginia. When she got there she was told that her aunt had died. While they couldn't let her see her aunt, they told her she was welcome to see the room that the woman had occupied. Mrs. Coe went to the room

and, tired after her journey, lay down on the bed for a nap.

She woke up to a doctor telling her she was to be transferred to another room. Mrs. Coe went with the doctor to the other room. She stayed in the hospital for 25 years before the mistake was discovered and she was discharged.

## Too Good

**H**ungarian hunter Endre Bascany was an expert at imitating the love call of a stag. Unfortunately, he was too good. One day in 1976 a hunter heard his call, thought it was a stag and fired, shooting Bascany in the arm.

## Dummies at War

**D**uring World War II, the Germans kept a close watch on troop movements in England. They

need not have bothered—many of the movements were faked by using dummies as troops.

## Marriage Mix-up

Albert Muldoon was the best man at the wedding in County Tyrone, Northern Ireland, but no one had told him where he should stand. He stood next to the bride. The priest assumed he was the groom and addressed all the questions to him. It was only after the service, when they went to sign the register, that the priest discovered he had married the best man to the bride. The ceremony had to be conducted again, this time with the groom and the best man in the correct places.

*The Wrong Place at the Wrong Time* 107

# 13 · Oh, No!

## Automatic Chaos

John Rimmer has good reasons to remember the day in 1985, when he first drove a car with automatic transmission. It happened in Liverpool, England. When John Rimmer stopped for gas, the service station attendant asked him to move his car back slightly. That's when the trouble began. John got his foot stuck between the accelerator and the brake pedal. The car shot backwards. The gas pump hose was caught, and pulled the pump over. The car door was open and caught the service station attendant, carrying him 20 yards

across the station. If that wasn't enough damage
for one day, the car then sped out into the road
and crashed into a parked car!

The gas station had to be closed down for the
day, and the service station attendant had to go to
the hospital. John Rimmer was not only fined and
penalized for careless driving, but he also lost his
job—as a driving instructor.

# Wrong Number

A lot of work went into compiling the new Paris
telephone directory issued in January 1983.
The French Telecommunications Ministry was
proud of its efforts—until someone pointed out
that the telephone number they had put down for
themselves was wrong!

# Easy Come—Easy Go

B uilders working on an extension to a hospital
in Mozambique in southeast Africa uncovered
a gigantic blunder when they knocked a hole
through a wall. On the other side they found a
fully-equipped maternity ward containing some
$75,000 worth of equipment. Workmen had appar-
ently walled up the ward by accident and hospital
authorities had forgotten it was there!

# Named In Error

In the early 1950s a woman was asked to launch a yacht in Bermuda. Twice she tried to break a bottle of champagne against its bows, but both times she failed. The boat slid down the slipway as the woman cried, "Oh, I can't!"

The yacht was therefore named *Oh I Cant!*

# Cracked It!

Stage star, Gertrude Lawrence, swung a champagne bottle to launch her cabin cruiser at Southampton in 1934, but the bottle missed. She tried again—and the ribbon broke. She then took the neck of the bottle in both hands and hit it against the bow of the vessel. Still, the bottle did

not break. Finally, she got an axe to smash open the bottle, and the cruiser was launched successfully.

## Wet Launch

Miss May Gould, a very determined Boston woman, was asked to launch a ship. When she tried to hit the vessel with the traditional bottle of champagne, the bottle missed and the ship slid away down the slipway.

But, Miss Gould was not about to leave the vessel un-named. She ran along the pier, dived into the water, smashed the bottle against the ship and named it from there.

# Strip Tease

The clerks at a Texas bank had quite a job on their hands. Thanks to a computer error, 200,000 incoming checks had been shredded. The clerks had to sort out the huge pile of thin strips of paper and put the checks back together!

# Atomic Disaster

Early in October 1976, Viennese radio in Austria gave out a frightening message: "Disaster at atomic power station—catastrophe warning. An atomic cloud driven by the wind is moving slowly towards the city." Parents rushed to schools to pick up their children; telephone lines were jammed and people set out on the roads to escape the approaching horror.

But it was all a mistake. The power station at Zwentendorf, 30 miles away, had not even started operations. The radio message was simply an exercise to find out what would happen if such a disaster were to occur.

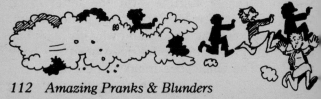

# 14 · It Almost Worked!

## Computerized Crime

A computer expert, working in a U.S. bank, devised an ingenious fraud. He ordered the computer to take just 10 cents from each customer's account and to transfer it to the last account on the record. He then opened an account with a surname starting with the letter Z. It worked well until a Mr. Zydel opened an account. Mr. Zydel could not understand why his bank balance kept increasing, so he questioned the bank about it. The employee's fraud was exposed.

*It Almost Worked!* 113

# Putting Couani on the Map

During the autumn of 1902, the President of Couani called a press conference at his luxury Paris hotel. Some of the reporters had never heard of Couani and, according to the President, Adolphe Brezet, that was the reason for the press conference. Brezet explained that Couani had long been dominated by its powerful neighbor, Brazil, but had now gained its independence. He had been sent to Paris to inform the world of its existence.

The President spoke so convincingly of his country that the reporters believed him, and by the end of the year everyone in Paris had heard of Couani.

Early in 1903, the first Couani embassy opened in Paris and this was soon followed by consulates in London, Rome, Berlin, and Madrid.

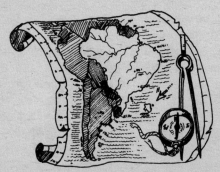

In 1904, Brezet had letters from both the Japanese and Russian governments. The two nations were at war and urgently needed more ships. Would it be possible, both nations wondered, for the famous Couani shipyards to build them? Brezet took a while to reply. Since such a delay was unusual for Brezet, the two countries checked up on Couani with their ambassadors in Brazil. Much to their surprise, they were informed that there was no such place! Brezet was not heard from again.

## Skullduggery

In 1912, Charles Dawson, an amateur geologist, was searching for specimens in a gravel pit on Piltdown Common in Sussex, England. He discovered flint tools, fossilized teeth and then parts of a human skull. Later it was estimated that the skull was 500,000 years old.

It was a great find for Dawson—but even greater treasures were in store. Later, with his friend Dr. Arthur Smith Woodward, he found part of a jaw. As this was unearthed near to the original find, they assumed that it came from the same person. But this could have been no ordinary person, because it had the jaw of an ape. And yet, the teeth had been ground down not as an ape's, but as human teeth are worn away. It seemed that here at last was the proof that humans were descended from apelike creatures. The skull and the jaw provided evidence of the so-called "missing link"—the link between humans and the apes.

The remains were displayed in the Natural History Museum in London and the "Piltdown Man" became famous throughout the world.

After a while, the Piltdown Man began to arouse suspicion. Evidence provided by other discoveries did not fit in with the ape man. By 1953 so much controversy surrounded the Piltdown Man that a more detailed examination of the remains was carried out.

As a result of this examination, an official announcement was made, on November 21, 1953,

declaring the Piltdown Man to be a fraud. It seems some of the tools found at the site had been aged artificially, and that the jaw of Piltdown Man had actually belonged to an orangutan. Even the skull was not as old as had first been thought.

One mystery still remains. It has never been proven who devised the fraud or why.

## The Cardiff Giant

Stubby Newell hired two men to dig a well at his farm near Cardiff, New York. They were surprised when they hit something solid about three feet underground. They cleared away the earth and to their amazement discovered the fossilized body of a giant man.

News soon got around about the incredible find. So many people wanted to see it that Stubby erected a tent over the site and charged visitors 50 cents a look. Some maintained that the giant was an ancient statue, but others believed it to be the fossil remains of a huge human.

Eventually, the Cardiff Giant was exhibited in the nearby town of Syracuse. Then the great showman, P. T. Barnum, never one to miss out on a money-making idea, commissioned some sculptors to carve a similar giant for his show. He called it "The Original Cardiff Giant." Both giants continued to draw crowds.

Barnum's giant was a fake—but what about the one found in Stubby Newell's field? Well, as was later discovered, that was a fake as well. It had been commissioned a year and a half before by George Hull, Stubby's cousin. Hull got the idea after hearing a preacher talk about the giants mentioned in Genesis in the Old Testament. The giant had been stained with sulfuric acid to make it look old and buried for a year to add "authentic" touches.

## Hughes Hoax

**H**oward Hughes, the eccentric millionaire industrialist, lived the life of a recluse and was seldom seen in public. When writer Clifford Irving

approached a publishing house claiming that Hughes had given him permission to ghostwrite his autobiography, the publishers, McGraw-Hill, were delighted. They agreed to pay a large advance sum to the millionaire and another sum to Irving. What they did not know was that Irving had already opened a Swiss bank account in the name of H.R. Hughes and took both sums himself.

Irving traveled the world on his ill-gotten gains. Whenever McGraw-Hill contacted him, Irving would say he had just finished another interview with the millionaire and that the book was coming alone fine.

Unfortunately for Irving, another hoaxer came up with the same idea and made a similar offer to a different publisher, who announced the fact. Naturally, McGraw-Hill instantly made it known

that they had already negotiated exclusive rights with the millionaire. The news got back to Hughes, himself, and a private detective was hired to investigate. It was not long before Irving's fraud was discovered.

## Portugal's Master Forger

**A**rthur Virgilio Alves Reis, an official in Portugal's colonial service, devised one of the most amazingly successful frauds of all time. In 1924 he discovered that the British printers, Waterlow and Sons, had printed some Portuguese bank notes. When he also found out that the Portuguese bank did not check for duplicate notes, he put his plan into action.

He sent an associate, Karel Marang, to London to negotiate with the printers. Marang took with him a forged document giving authority for money to be printed using the same plates and the same serial numbers as the previous order, for use in the African state of Angola. Official documents presented to the printers stated this would not cause any confusion in Portugal as the notes were to be overprinted with the name "Angola" when they reached Africa.

The notes were printed, and Reis and his accomplices smuggled them into Portugal. It took

almost a year for the government to realize that there were a large number of 500-escudo notes in circulation. Investigators were sent to the banks to find out what was happening. When they searched the Bank of Angola and Metropole,

which had been set up by Reis, they found packets of the new notes.

Reis was arrested, but because the documents he had forged were so expertly done, it was five years before he could be tried. He was eventually sentenced to 20 years in prison. Two of his accomplices also received prison sentences and a third fled the country.

## Caught by Computer Failure

An employee of a Minnesota bank programmed its computer to ignore any checks drawn on his account. The fraud worked quite well—until the computer broke down and his crime was discovered.

# Lost in the Mist

Arthur Bottomley, an English con man, devised what appeared to be a foolproof way of winning a lot of money at horse racing.

He made sure that he owned all six horses in a race in Blankenburg, Belgium, but pretended that they were all owned by different people. The jockeys were told in which order they were to finish. Bottomley hired several people to place bets for him.

The scheme seemed perfect, but once the race had started, a thick mist blew in from the sea. The jockeys lost sight of each other in the fog and eventually crossed the finishing line in the wrong order.

# Humbert's Inheritance

When Therese Humbert heard groans coming from the locked railway compartment next to hers, she bravely climbed along the outside of the train to see what she could do. In the compartment she found a man who had just had a heart attack. She climbed in and helped him. The man, Robert Henry Crawford, said he would be eternally grateful to her for saving his life and would reward her one day.

Two years later, in 1881, Therese received a letter saying that Crawford had died and made her a beneficiary in his will. The will said that Therese was to look after Crawford's family fortune, which was locked in a safe, until her younger sister,

Marie, was old enough to marry one of Crawford's two nephews.

The story of the inheritance enabled Therese and her husband to obtain loans and improve their life style. Eventually they had to take out larger loans to cover the interest on the original loans. For 20 years, the Humberts lived in luxury, in spite of attempts to discredit Therese's story. But by 1902, the bankers suspected that the amount of the inheritance might not be enough to cover all the loans and legal costs. They insisted on opening the safe. When it was opened, the authorities were amazed to find that it contained only a brick and an English halfpenny. By this time the Humberts had disappeared. They were arrested in Madrid in December 1902.

Therese was jailed for five years and her two brothers, who had played the fictitious nephews of the non-existent Robert Crawford, were sentenced to two and three years each.

# The End

**P**aintings by Raphael Boronali were greeted by the art world as masterpieces when they first appeared in Paris in 1977. The paintings turned out to have been "painted" by a donkey with a paintbrush attached to its tail!

# Index